AF583285

The Potion Store

Hypno

THE POTION STORE

ISBN: 979-888641102-7

Dedication

For my Mother & Father.

Visit

In 2016, opened a store in an alley in NY, just like any other thing in the world, it was just an idea. The streets usually stay filled with a cold breeze. The owner of the store liked to describe it as 'warm under the blanket season.'
On July 17, a young lad visited the store he was wearing her grandmother's handmade sweaters he opened the old shabby door of the store and took a look at the inside of the duplex: A complete wooden, glossy, and heart comforting warm. He then slowly closed the door and took few steps inside as his eyes got a hold of the big spiral stairs following their way up to another floor. He looked for the owner, but there was no one at the desk. He uttered slowly, 'Hello?' But no reply came. He then hears a screeching voice as the two bookshelves slide in the opposite direction and a man in his late forties comes out. He looked like a person who had aged like a bottle of wine.

His pure white sweater and smell that one would say came straight from heaven. He looked down at the young kid and greeted him, "Goodmorning! Young man." The kid couldn't say a word, the man said, "It's completely fine young chap a lot of people nowadays lose words over attractive people, I'm glad you lost yours over me, don't worry consider yourself home."

Let me show you around he said, as they walked forward inside the shop. He opened an old wooden door beyond that it was all surreal. It was all the pieces made by that man entire his life. The kid asked, Is it all yours? He replied, "It was, but now I want to share all of this with the world." He added, let me show you something very special to me he took him through that big spiral stair to another floor, there was a big window, and the view from that showed Manhattan covered in all snow.
The kid was awe-struck, the man asked him to press a red button. So, he did anxiously and slowly a vault opens, hammer-like spotlight comes down on a white book. He took the book out of the vault and tells him "This book right here was written when I was close to your age. It summarizes my 5 years of experience from that time. In this book, my child there lies a story of a person who believed more in creating magic than in waiting for it to happen. I want you to read it."

Right after handing the book to the kid, the man disappeared by the time he could look up to ask, "Is it all written by you it says, 'Is that ass up for grabs?'"

There was no trace of him like he vanished in thin air, down on the floor he found a newspaper with the front line, “Famous poet from 'written on white' opened his first ‘Potion Store’ in NY, visitors claim magic still exist!”

The kid took the book and the newspaper and headed back to his home. That night it rained heavily, he sat in his study desk, which was close to a window the raindrops slid down as he tuned to some lo-fi hip-hop radio and pulled the book from his bag and turned to the first page;

As the narrator twisted the story and put reality to it, you my friend are the reader of that pure white book consider yourself the first one who got something just by reading about it. I'm delighted that you got this book, I would like to welcome you to this journey that leads to no bounded road, limits crossed, and feels unexplored.

Some of the pieces are empty, I din’t bother to complete them because I want you to write your own story in it.

Tune in to some Lo-fi just like that kid and let’s read this together just so you know you are not alone.

PEOPLE: Somethings I like to keep alive only in the theory now.

HYPNO

BEGINNING

Let's begin from when I first started to feel a little more. This was when our annual day practice started for the first time. The event was quite distinct itself from rest. The same place we hated turned out to be the foremost. It was chiefly due to the timing, I assume now. We were called at the time when they used to let us off. From being woken up early in the morning sleepily dragging our asses to the bus, It was much more convenient. Every child at least once thinks of going to his school in the night time.

'We were in that concept which only saw sunlight coming in the astrodome.' It was the first time we were about to see it shimmer down on us. After our practice, we used to sit in pacts & play 'King, Ministers & Thief ' that friendship never seemed that beautiful when we were under that night sky as it does now when we are heading toward life and now these nights keep on taking tolls.

But none of this was special to me except that last bus ride home every day. The city shimmers as it gets dark outside, the cold wind in my face from the window. Some kind of euphoric feeling, Years down later now I named it 'HYPNOTIC'. Yet, I don't know what it is and maybe somewhat that's what it is all about; to be lost in a feeling you never had before.
But for the first time, I felt like a grown-up like I was on my own going out somewhere in the middle of the night with no one to tell me how to live it right.

Do you remember when you first felt like being
grown-up?

This is before, I asked my heart to quit.

вино и поэзия
wine and poetry

In the search of her presence
I reached her home where she used
to live with her lover; she was long gone from
there and I was moved past on in my life
for this to bother me
or at least I thought I did.
The idea of her being somewhere
in my close proximities still brings out a series of
sensations sometimes puts a grasp around my heart
and when I assume it's her in the crowd what my eyes
just saw that hold gets strong enough to make
the heart go skip a beat.
“Time' what it takes to heal from a person is pretty
uncertain.”
Even after a year or two there are parts of you that
remained stuck in me also, after a year or two there is
a whole lot, I've moved on from.
//
Magic is when you start understanding what's good
for you and what's not.
Listen to your instincts, always!
I would like to welcome y'all to, ‘The Book of Potions’;
This is my life experience in my own words.

Early morning rains
with willing to sleep for longer girlfriend
and bed tea providing boyfriend.

She's one of those who make
Louis V's, double C's look good.
Cold like ice running in her veins,
heart comforting warm even
when it rains.

Jefferson St.

Miss Jeff, she lived in an apt. on Brooklyn Street with her cat Filicia. Miss Jeff, she had a habit of smoking cigarettes in the early morning while playing light jazz music. She used to slightly turn up the volume while letting the lobbies get filled up by soft interludes as she sips her black tea and fills her journal. I recently moved to NY next door to her. The sound of her jazz machine caught me in the morning. One day, I followed the consonance, which led me to her room.

She was a kind soul. She invited me over and offered me a latte. I asked her, "If she was doing okay, all that music and cigarettes?" She said, "People are confined to them, they want to be reached out but they hesitate to ask somewhere deep down I feel if this can open a window for them. Doing a little extra for someone goes a long way." She also added, *"People conflate things, when they don't need so much to get by. I used to write hand-written notes on restaurant papers as a memoir to keep it safe in a book somewhere and I was happy with that alone. You do what you love and continue it till you love it."*

At first, it reminded me of that girl who used to hold people's hands for 5 bucks when they asked her why she does so? She replied, because I don't have anyone to hold hands with either. She was just clever enough to make a buck out of it. But I was sitting there thinking what a day to be alive experiencing someone living a little extra for others. She was the kind to pull out a rose first in a knife fight, the type that will make you wonder what a person has to go through to be this wise.

"ever felt like taking a drive down the hill
at 2 am with someone you can't take your
eyes off and talk almost about whatever
while the radio playing your favorite jam
with showers of rain adding its own melody
to it and you're just lost in a feeling you
never had before."

On a rainy day. In a home. Out of thoughts.

&

Sitting next to a potful of coffee fantasizing with all the dreamy ideas you getting about love that you can do to someone. By this time, you are already half in love.

Disclaimer:

Things like this can make you more romantic.

RAIN

These light rains are the favorite go out's. The feel of tickling cold drops under your sweatshirt. Look how everything has a tinted vibrance now, pluck flowers give them to random people, tell 'em they look beautiful, be a kid with a kid, sit on a building cliff embracing the cold winds. Let them strangle your hair. See the city gets painted by the rain drops, dance on your favorite tunes. Go back in the streets, sit with strangers and listen to their love stories, ask about their journey from B&W to hue. Find different places and don't stop. It's still raining and it hasn't stopped yet.

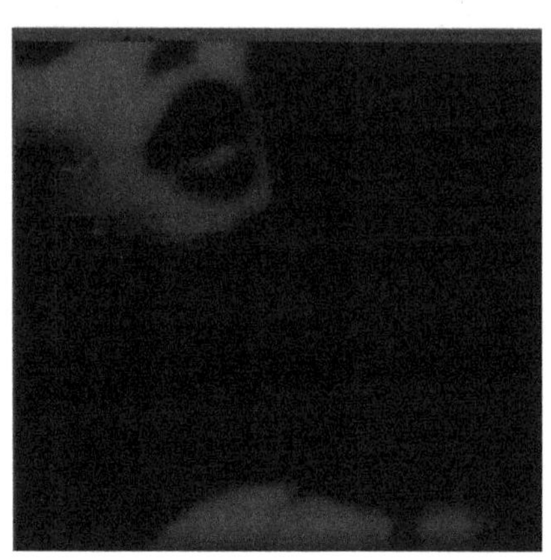

Rose-tinted lights are the drive

with her voice so soft, words so cold &

a heart so pure that you don't want to

play in affection.

// let love shall be the traction.

"You're my kind of quiet."

Soft-spoken but cold on words making use of them only when needed otherwise your silence last durations. Some consider it rude; I consider you aren't worth the time to express what's on the mind, doodling on rooftop with headphones blaring, sitting there looking astonshing, waiting there not to be found.

Late-night coffee with rain sliding down
the windowpane as I read poetry and talk
about love like that's all I've ever known.

//

"It's never leaving when you got each other in your thoughts."

KEEP THIS
TICKET
★ YOU MAY WIN A PRIZE ★
№ 143875J
25 c

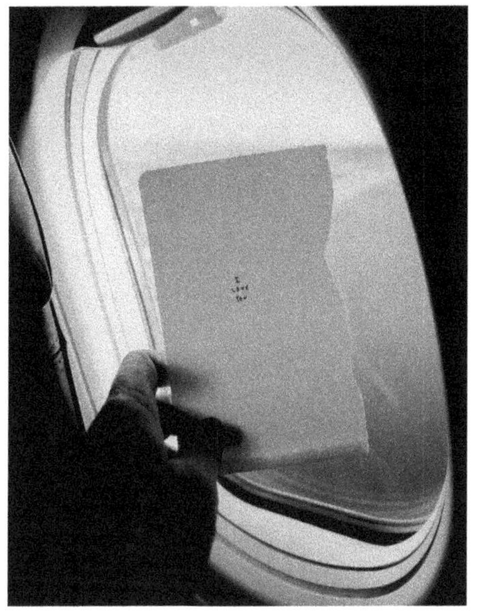

"In a world full of texts send someone a letter."

"Years from now on things will be a lot different, you'd be living a life you didn't know about. And one day, you will be hit by nostalgia reminding you of all the things that came and went. Things that stayed & became a part of your journey. Somethings are so smooth they brush away so swiftly you never come to know, these are those smooth days. Fast forward and now as you living that mainstream life, doing 9–5 job, having a responsibility to put food on the table and a mouth to feed. But tonight, It's just about that nostalgia, and when it hits you, take the time out to remind yourself with every beautiful memory that you ever came across, every single person who put a glimpse in your timeline. Sometimes I do wonder if someone will remember the guy who used to 'write on the white...?'"

The thought that after a year or two
we'll never be able to meet. But by the
time that day comes I want to have
one last open heart to heart talk with
you but the fact that you don't want me
back
I think I just have to leave it here.

SOMETHINGS ARE

BETTER NOT KNOWN,

SOMETHINGS ARE BETTER

LEFT ALONE.

// I'm words that will love you when they won't.

Me: Mum, where did you keep my black hoodie
I'm looking for it in my shelf & I can't find it and
I only found my one sock who took the other one?

Mom: *arrives* looks in the same cupboard and pulls out both my hoodie and socks with some extra useful stuff that I never knew I had.

Me: How do you...Like every time??

"What can I write for Mom?
I am Mom's writing."

Come at midnight wearing an oversized black hoodie with classic Vans on, smelling Light Blue Dolce & Gabbana asking for a city surf and make the heart go drive down the hill.

I don't take
compliments like they
aren't for me but I love
myself like there is no
special being.

"Driving down the hill in my Monte Carlo still feels the same when we kissed for the first time, the tension between these lips, revving it close enough just not to meet the edge 'til we actually hit the e-brake and our lips difted together to meet a match."

"Lighten up on perfect,
It's the flaw I'm trying to
make you fall in love with."

"Even if I crashed it's still going to be art."

Polaroids, Super 8 they always had something; the world captured in it always looked so friendly.

If I had to go back in time, I would go to the era where VHS, polaroid, Super 8 was used to capture the moments. They say, "Super 8 was a language of silence." I won't deny, everyone had the same 8mm film with their own recorded footage and everyone had a different story to their film.

They only had like 20 shots in a polaroid film, unlike today's camera. So, 'every shot was a world'. Capturing was almost like creating a moment back then. Lastly, capture every footage when you can (more videos than pictures) because people will leave like it or not but you'll have something to cherish when you won't be able to walk & that something of today will make you feel better tomorrow. And you will be proud at least you lived when you had the time.

"There's always risk in living my
friend, you still do it.
Make it count."

"I would'nt told you if revealing wasn't the best part about mystery."

"GIVE YOURSELF THE STRUGGLE YOU NEED FOR THAT FLEX."

It's up to you.
You can lay in bed all-day
and watch the world gets created by
others and spend your whole life
appreciating or disagreeing with what
they do.
Or you can contribute a part of yourself
by completely devoting to what you believe and
leave a piece of you before you leave this earth.
It's always you.
"Do it before going to the grave."

CLIMBING MORE THAN YOU CAN ROLL

.

I understand all nights are not the same.
Some nights are sleep chasing, guilt taking,
blame throwing, eroding in self-loathing asking
for the things to have remained the same /
mayhem till the AM’s.

I strongly believe that some people are made for
more than just the idea of giving and receiving love.
Their purpose is alot more bigger than that.

It's up to you
I'm striving hard every day just to make it.
But I know it’s a lie what I'm doing is not
enough. Some nights are like that they are not
meant to sleep. And this ‘keep you awakened all
night feeling’ of yours will likely turn out into the
nothingness of tomorrow.
Choose wisely.

Hello!

Yes ?

I know you've not been doing
okay lately, the plants
you watered din't grew, the
love you gave 'em din't
brew but it's okay. I'm here
to take you out for a coffee
that might end up on a
rooftop
venting all the caffeine out.
Counting the stars,
gazing the moon
and losing our souls in each
others words. Forgetting our
problems and diving
into something they call
"Complete".

"Its just words until it comes from the right person then it's all 'Magic.'"

"You'll find me in every street named after love."

The last two digits of their cellphone number still brings out a series of sensations in you. That's how I also want to be remembered in people's hearts: little bit nervous and a whole lot excited.

Not so virgin thoughts yet pure just like

Among all the boys you don't haunt me
neither you want to change a thing about me yet,
at the same time inspire me to be the better
version of myself.
That's what I like about you. You are better off
with creating your world that also brings the
best out of other people & that's what
I love you for.

Me & her:

"Two highs can't come down."

Love at second sight.
first was just dope.

ALL I

DO IS

WRITE

POETRY

AND

THINK

ABOUT

HER.

you want magic ?
try
Truth!

When the mood is on me
lewd is not the scene
just blackout a city candle lit
the streets &
call for your favorite peeps.

"I only make love sound good; I don't guarantee it."

With me it's like a drive down the hill: thrilling, beautiful and something you never had before.

CAPTURE

THE

ESSENCE

OF

BEING

UNBOTHERED.

My heart is for a girl who is hiding somewhere in the shadows.

"When you smile so genuine
it clicks. Next time you
drink coffee think about
me."

Café in street,
viscose textured latte's.
French girl with French toast
doodling her new friends on
napkins to
keep a memoir
for all the things;
all the could's and have
been's.

"You only do those things to others
that you wish someone else would've
done for you."

Like remember the time you put a smile
on someone else's face when you were the
one who needed it the most.

"I CANNOT THINK WHAT KEEPS HIM SO."

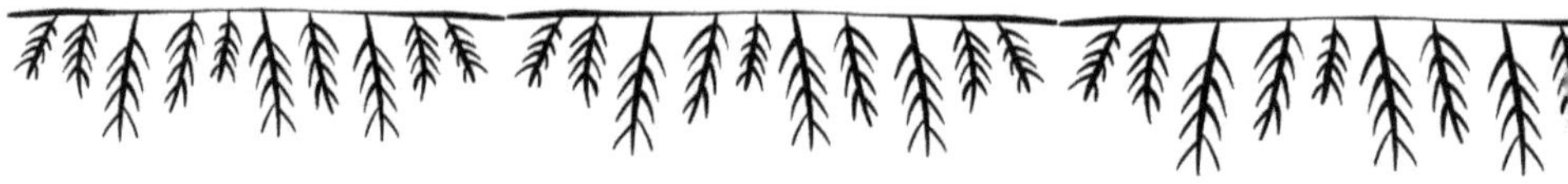

Christmas is about that warmness you'd be getting with your favorite people. You'll experience the best Christmas spirits in schools, streets, churches and near a person who keeps a little something extra to make the world feel slightly magical / better than before. It's ‘warm under the blanket season’. Go grab some hot drinks with your favorite peeps.

I love dalhia for it blushes
in all the right places.

I will draw rainbow on both of your cheeks
and then comparing it with you I would say, “A lot more than this, that's how much beautiful you make my life.”

I like my girl cold for the world
and warm for me.

When I first saw her,
I was scared. I thought
she might lose herself,
people will make
fun of her, 'Cuz what
she lacked was:
Prettiest eyes,
girly hairs, perfect body,
a melodious voice;
pretty much what your
eyes were looking for
but what she had
was something
a million girls out
there might lack
" A fl a w loving
personality "
She embraced her flaws
more tightly than people
ever did it with their perfection
That's what made me
realise that the most
exotic flowers b l o o m
in the most care-free world.

POTION: Self realization

"Never go back to them who made you miss yourself instead of them."

Imagine being whole and still missing out on someone. It takes several tries to understand your extra love toward someone does not turn red flags into a green one just because you have the mental and emotional strength to love more won't make them love you more.

The first day or last the person mostly remains the same either you like them or like something they have there is nothing in between.

"With love but without excluding the reality."

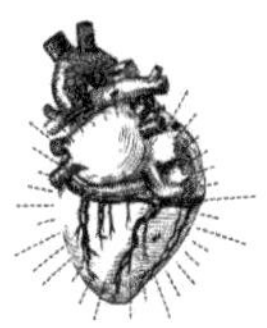

"My heart behind the wheel
is terrible, it never takes that
'Hard-right'."

Parking lot

When it comes to shitty
people I get a lot like
where cars park.

If possible I would've
loved me from your side
too but I guess that's not
how it works,
that's not how love works.

You were wrong
at picking someone right.

It's okay.

happens.

It's alright.

Same stories will be repeated again
with different names, with different
faces on different locations & with
better heart's this time.

just hold on

A muse

"It's for my own muse that I write
and subconsciously for yours too."
I don't want to take all the benefits from
these words alone, so I share these with you.
I don't mind who is going to get much bigger
with this so, I just wish you use these better,
as your ladder for your get-ups.
But I'm happy at least I'm able to
give because no 'give is in me.' So, that gives up
the chances of me giving up!
But as you rise up in this fame you got ticks ready to
suck up your name we lovingly call them as critics
in this game, they trying to tell you writing these 4 lines
and getting diminished afterward is not
enough, it's darn they term it as 'Instapoetry' to depict us
as lame.

In other words, It's too naive for the real world.
Funny! People who think they have acquired higher
knowledge of words but can't write one of their own
can predict what's good and worse for all.
The narrative is naive poetry got me more answers
about the real world than your ancient text could.
It's all good poetry as long as you fit the writer's
shoes and learn something from it. So, scoot when it
doesn't & don't tell me about the things we've been through,
you didn't help us find a way to get out of the
places we were put through.
There were other options too could've picked up a
gun and went ambrose.
But you should be more scared, I picked up a pen boo &
you don't want to see the flipside of this book, It will be:
'How I'll be your Schitzo.'
So, appreciate when I say:
"I heal when I write and I'm happy if you heal from it too."
That's what every writer would want that their readers
heal from their healings, but then again
"It's for my own muse that I write
and subconsciously for yours too."
So, enjoy your stay because mine is going to last even
after you.

—

"If you don't know how to make
love stay then this too shall pass."

Neither your negligence
nor your affection make
sense to me anymore.

-At eternal peace

Can't keep?
Can't stay.

Alone?
No problem.
But on the
top, on a
throne.

Romance-

-By H. Stratton

"Rage rage till the dying of light,
got weeps to sweep and smiles to rise."
Girl said, "You so write so Beaut,
You should take me to the fly.
O' boy, O' boy, you so great you should
land in my life."
Boy said, "If I so great I should only land
in myself.
O' girl, O' girl, you only look pretty standing
from a sight."

"Just star gazing in people."

It was like living in Paris
with having you by my
side,
a view so scenic you don't
want to reroute,
you used to come in my
room embracing all my
problems away till you
became the problem &
went away.

Losing

On some nights I'm just
trying to hold on to you
you grew distant so fast &
slowly I've been losing these
memories and I don't want to
forget about you & what it felt
when we were together.

I think, "you think alot about me"
faded up a little too quickly.

"It still comforts my heart talking about you even long after you are gone."

Kudos to everyone who hides everything so well even though their heads been a crash scene and nobody gives a damn about it.

“Maybe that's what it is for some: Loving unconcerned.”
We were too comfortable together and they say, ‘You should get out of your comfort zone.’ is maybe why we didn't last.

I did every bit of myself to forget about you,
I somehow succeeded at that, I even outdid myself
because it was tough to forget about you compared
to any other human. I remember our endless talks felt
great and I don’t even remember what we talked about,
I remember your face but not the details of what
it felt like to hold you.
I forgot about you, but also it’s hard to write now.

"So many books are written in the name of love for someone who didn't know how to love back."

When you are happy, you will just flip through these pages like they don't mean much to you, similar to the first day of meeting with the person you didn't know you'll end up falling in love with. But look at the magic it will bring to you when you are falling apart on those nights where staying away meant staying awake. You will then linger on every page, every word, like you are dying right now to hold your lover who's long gone and I'm sorry about that, like I'm not writing all this because of the same. So, this is for that time.

And, sometimes you do need a better understanding of being able to see it from both sides & what it's like to be in their shoes too, because *sometimes it's not always about you.*

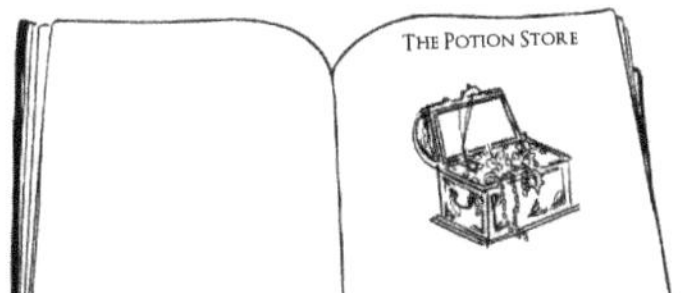

THE POTION STORE

"Being sad is overrated too."

Cliché; not my type.

If not then,

"Why don't you talk about love nowadays
when you like to talk about rare things?"

Rhapsody still a delphic story

I don't know how we collide with each other.
But I remember that we went on a walk. And, it
eventually started raining. We ran to a close by shed,
watching it pour we started walking opposite
to each other waiting for it to stop is when
we first started talking about ourselves.
For the first time, you told a lot about yourself
hours went by, but the conversation was not ready
to die.

I'll never forget it,
from that day forward, the conversation never really
stopped even after years it still felt the same between us,
we got nothing but close to each other over time.
"Loving you was not the best thing, getting loved by you
was." Missing on all the small gestures that you did to me
but like all good things it also had an end maybe your
mask fell off and I just couldn't keep picking it back up
again & again just to make me realize that, 'It's not 'you'
with the mask off'. So, I had to leave for my heart.
It's funny that ever since then, I don't really seem to find it
now in me much. The truth is we din't loved each other. We
were just there. But I was not ready to leave because I never
thought it would even be an option.
Two years have passed by and I've never heard from her,
barely seen her either.
The only time I feel weak is when my words can't
bring out enough magic to bring her back to me.

"I hope you come out as I painted you in my imagination & not like some other from the reality."

"Sometimes I wonder that a page is much better as a listener no matter how bad my writing is or how many flaws I have in my grammar. It doesn't judge me for what it is or who I am and yet still gives me clarity to rewrite my mistakes, It lets me be me. I think maybe that's what people also want on some days: just to be heard not to be judged, interfered or changed, to be loved and given credit for what they are instead of what they should be."

"It's hard to write about you after you are gone, especially when I'm moving on."

In amidst cold winds, showers of gentle rain
and fog taking over, making the vision go in
vain is when I found you.
You complimented the weather so much
you disappeared in the same.
Maybe you didn't like to stay at one place with the
same people. And maybe you think of me as weak
because I don't have anyone by my side, but don't
you feel powerless in other people's ride
who are you when separated from their shine?

Keep some flowers for yourself.

I can’t always keep saving, you see.
Doing too much for too many; bad decision.

Honey, It’s okay to trip
sometimes afterall
you’re growing.

This world made me forget about my happiness until I took a fall, learned to stand on my own and chose to create it. But it was at the cost of losing 'believe' in a lot of people, even to those I considered friends but they never were, had to give up on all of that.

Just to do something of my own that will bring me happiness and in hope that will also bring a person alongside with it like I don't even know if any of it is even true.

But just believe it when I said, 'I gave up on people.'

A random quote

Sometimes it's hard to explain why / what you are the way you are and sometimes you just rely on some random quote which can do it better for you.

'You'

Sitting here writing for the realism.
Lands combined, seas dried;
stretched together to form a vast land.
To fit as many inhabitants as it can.
Yet, only one voice inside.

The questions you ask and the answers
you receive are only from yourself,
even the most scorching individuals
I doubt if they don't do the same.
No matter how big the world is
they all talk to them.
So, what's the difference between
us all? How do some just make it?
While others keep on floating from
Past to Present to Past.

When deep down we know
all we have is 'us' &
there is no doubt in that then
why don't we do things only for
ourselves?
Out of the feelings for once,
And focus on the things we must.

"Care only for yourself !"
Everyone says that nowadays, including me in some of my write-ups. But now when I think about it more isn't it making the world more lonelier? We human species like to have interactions based on who we are. But since no body is listening or reaching out to anyone, It's just creating a void in us for the long term which not only we carry but also pass on just because somebody betrayed us or broke our heart. We became too scared to make another attempt & hid ourselves in a nutshell. Once a surgeon said to me, "If you are going out of your home, there's risk of getting hit by something and you take that risk."

Maybe life is all about that. If you want something, you got to put a part of yourself on the line. It's not about, 'not caring for yourself or hiding from the world'. It's about finding the balance.

"The art of doing what's right for the moment."

In her home of figmentation
I was putting in bricks of reality
having no clue, she was building her
own platform 9¾ on the inside.

"Honey, if he will mean it
you'll see it in his eyes."

"Those lips tasted the best with coffee on them."

I don't share my friends.
-Type of person

"A lost wanderer for the most beautiful smile."

I hope in the end
it's of no one else
but your own.

The procedure to
unravel the bricks of
my heart
is to keep
constantly bugging
me with your
kindness.

"Linger on honesty regardless of the chaos it brings."

If it was for me I would'nt have done it.
But if it was for you I would've
done it twice.

This is how you stab yourself.

Lost in translation

I waited for you in silence
I din't wanted to tell anyone what I felt.
But maybe I should've broadcasted the
message. So, it could've reach you.

You'll find me in places not filled with a
lot of crowd, I like my places where not
everyone can make it. Sometimes you can
find me sitting in laundry rooms blaring
music, sippin' caffeine. You can always
visit me you know. You can ask me out for a
coffee if you have a heart interwine with
pure reefs. And, I only like my coffee
cold until it snows I guess.
I hope it'll be not easy to forget about me
& I hope this is somewhere you'll always
find me before we catch a distance that
we cannot cover. I hope you keep this book
close to you always.
But honestly keep me closer than the book
itself because words might get lost in the
translation but I want to stay, close to
everyone who has ever loved me and never
swayed their way.

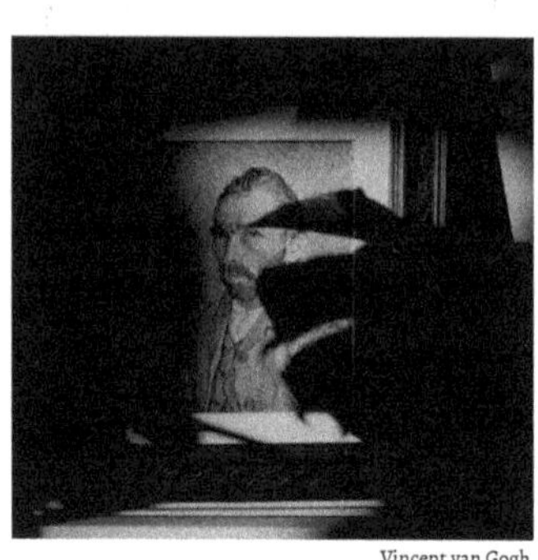

Vincent van Gogh

"To avoid yourself from drought stop pouring water into others."

For the dark thoughts running wild in
you that the world ignored.
I admire that.
so come
along,
I care.

“I'm that person who'll get away from things as soon as they become *cliché*.”

A poet's fall
can be
a little
terrible for the readers.

You just use other people to
forget other people.

-we are not alike.

"Your lips travel more than I do."
It's just you do people and I do places.

&

The only word I think before 'you'
now is 'fuck'.

"The funny thing about
chasing the past
is no one
actually lives there."

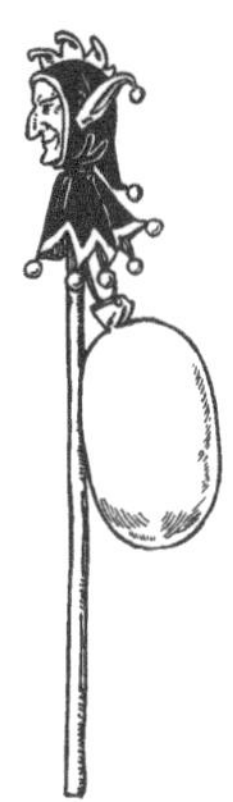

This time you ain't cheating my heart,
'cuz this time I'm playing the
liar.

"I don't need to remove my clothes
to make you feel things. If you are a
strip down I'm the wind in the rain
*I'm not that feeling that's gonna go
away.*"

"All those empty places
wanted someone to be
there."

They say people come and go all the time
'So, is making attachments a wrong thing or being
heartless is the key?'

——

"Either you wait for them to love you
or you just love yourself back."

There's a certain amount of percentage that you can change a person and no matter what that number is, It's always less compared to changing yourself. So, I would say stop painting colors on others that fascinate you, 'you won't change theirs' instead paint yourself gold, point a finger to yourself and rewire 'your wire'. Work for the betterment. *And if you ask me the percentage that you can change in someone else, I'll say 0.*

Behind our screens,
we all are *l o s t*
people who are
trying to find
solace in a relatable poetry.

Holding down the phone late at night
scrolling through our galleries watching the same
memories from different POV's that we don't
share anymore
unfortunately.

Or fortunately I don't know.
Alot has changed, So I wish the good in you.
This might be an incomplete piece because so was our
story but maybe some other time, will go for another
nightout in some other city.
Till then peace x

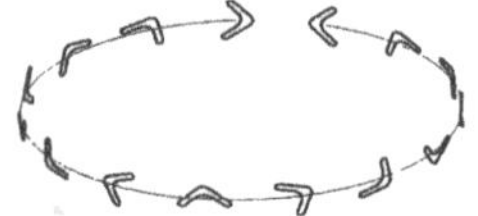

"I don't know much about
love except for the part that
it's a good place to be 'where
it comes back too'."

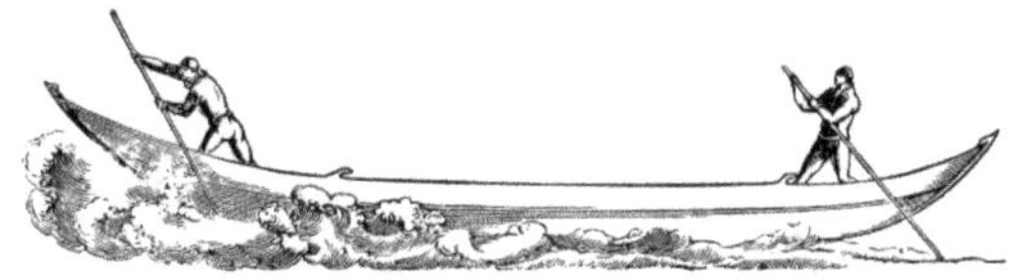

Don't bring yourself to
a situation where you won't be
able to move without them;
We'll set our own
amplitude, we'll become
our own tide.

"We will flow in our pavement."

“'Long time no see..?'
Same things I say about love.”

//

“Showing love should never be a problem in a world where nothing is guaranteed.”

I'll be that taste
you want to
leave but can't
rather be tea or
nicotine I don't care.

And the story never
told that there was
someone who put that
smile on her face.

"I was young, drunk and full of love but..."

She was never mine to keep, So I have no right to feel. The feeling of: abandonment, jealousy, regret, left out, not worthy enough for being someone's lover, all this is not for me. I just have to remember all she was my best friend that got intimately connected with the chemistry of mind and body, close enough to understand the unsaid. Yet, that doesn't justify why she one day found someone, fell for his attractiveness and left me all of a sudden. That's true she was not bounded by anything so she could! Leave me whenever she liked, all I ever was, was just a best friend right..? So, It's a bestfuckin' end right?
Maybe yes.
So, I just have to remind myself every day that I don't have the right to feel anything for her.

"She wanted to leave so I let her go, she didn't want me to come back so, I never came back."

"I was drunk when I said, I care for you."
-But you don't drink.

~~MEN DON'T CRY.~~
MEN DON'T MAKE WOMEN CRY.

Met a man at the substation today, he asked,
“How are things going?”
I said, ‘Going.’ He replied, “It's all
made up you see: the words, these stories, their
promises, the rides they take with you. It's all till
something better comes on.
The more you will grow in your life, the more you
will realize, ‘There is no place for emotions &
things perform in a logical way’.”
He added, “But one thing is real, ‘You till
yourself.’ So, when
you say things are going, let them.
Just hold on to yourself.”

In the need of me
filling my taste from
several shall not be your
eternal; from feeling
loved
will become to
not being able to
love anyone.

If I am supporting you
but have to find someone else
for my support then this ain't
the thing
either get it right or get left.

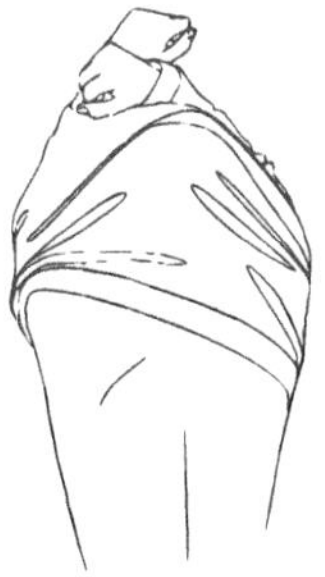

"People undress with the lies.
with all intentions to make it a look 'alike'."

"I'm the road and I'm leading
it to the places I want to go,
your concern is what I'm not concerning."

Never a RELATIONSHIP

I reached a point in life
being everyone's
everything:
The best to go out with, best friend, best care-
giver the phrase itself burns me down now
like you are the ‘hoe’.
But, I'm acting a ‘people pleaser’
both ways we are getting
fucked. For what?
Just to end up
regretting and venting
it out here;
always everyone's
everything but never a
relationship!

"Last time I loved so hard I had to apologize."

I literally feel like you could die with a
"*Should I?*"
Don't give shit to people who just
sits and take.

I'm a poem myself
too deep to bring on the
surface and too short
to put in words.

Tell 'em I sit on
hills, playing harp
emitting happiness.

After a span of 3 years 5 of us sat
together, we opened bottles, shared
some laugh, removed our masks
kept it
on the table & talked, it was a good talk.

" It's *c a l m* after the storm
beautiful stories are after the *c h a o s* ."
//
The sailor of the ocean says: There's depth in you, you just can't die when you have the power to generate tides within people. You haven't even traveled to the duskiest roads or climbed the greenest hills.

Your story is yet to be written.

It's silly to ask If I did that
for me or you?
Or was leaving
a good option to any of us?

The wise: To both.

"I wonder If my writings
will ever become someone's
reason to begin a
conversation?"

“Let blur, seeing what needs to be seen.”

how many lives / nights
you have ruined by loving
people & then walking
away keeping them
wondering
all their lives if they weren't good enough.

Aratus Cilix
Ptolemeus Aegyptius
Azophi Arabus
Thaurus
Aries
Caput medusæ
Deltoton
Pisces
Perseus
Andromeda
Cassiopea
Erichthonius
Gemini
Pegasus
Vrsa maior
Cancer
Vrsa minor
Cepheus
Equiculus
Aquarius
Capricornus
Delphinus
Sagitta
Lyra
Leo
Draco
Aquila
Hercules
Ophiuchus
Sagittarius
Bootes
Corona
Anguis
Virgo
Libra
Scorpio

"They say, "In a battle of egos, losers win." But you have to take on board the difference between ego and self-respect. Do not feel sorry for your efforts if the same amount is not being reverted; always have the strength to leave the table."

I have become an empty city
all these places give a sense of longing,
all these streets feel empty like we were the
only Mr. Hustle & Ms. Bustle to them!
These shops are also on the verge of shutting down.
There's still a little hope left in me as we still live
in the same city.
Maybe one day one of us will reach out to the other
and the visitor will not meet with any anger just a
long-awaited hug saying,
“I'm glad you came because I never would’ve
had the strength to do that.”
I hope that day comes early
and tonight,
I just hope to fall asleep
before I fall apart.

One day we both crossed each
other's path. We looked at each
other for a second or two just to
make sure, It was the right
one to ignore.

MAKE THEM KISS A BOTTLE / JEALOUSY POTION

#1 Find a connection depending on your fate / looks / personality / efforts..etc

#2 This potion works best when your partner is inferior to you in looks. So, their chances of finding someone attractive are already reduced to half making you have an upper hand.

#3 In the starting days of your relation reduce the amount of your self-respect and pour two big table spoons of attention and mix them well. They are too ugly to understand if it's all real at first and will start to feel on top.

#4 Bingo! Now you're ready to give them a taste of it. Call them in the middle of the night and start pouring out some tears on the phone call and tell them something sad that recently happened to you, which is not even sad to other people but when you'll call them in the middle of the night and act as if you can only share this with them, they will feel more confident about themselves and as they being the nice persons / assholes they will start to comfort you as if it's not something to be worried about. They will call your name in their *trying to impress voice* trying to win you. From there, you can enter their personal mind space.

#5 Now that you've reached their sensitive spot, just keep adding to the game, you can set doses according to yourself: Go out with them, drink coffee, make food together. And when you're ready to kill add sex, start teasing that will make them hard to resist, they will act strongly like that shit doesn't bother them, and right before you go any further say on the first spot, “You don't love them and they shouldn't fall in love with you.” This will leave them silent, their egos will get hurt for a while, then you reduce the dose by saying this excuse that, “You are not ready for any sort of relationship in this period of your life.” This will ensure that the problem is not with them and they will understand your space because of course assholes, I mean nice people.

#6 Now you're all set you got the fish hooked now you can play accordingly however you want the outcomes to be. Keep making ‘em comfy in the upcoming months so, they almost forget the difference b/w a relation and FWB. After that, start giving pain shots by reminding them that they shouldn't get attached to them. Do it better by your actions: Go drinking with your friends, go to other people’s parties they are introverts, so who will call them or even if someone does, they will not go. Now whatever you'll do is bad for you & they'll just keep on caring for you telling that it's not good for you and your future.

#7 Keep going like this and one day find another guy in this same manner then tell the old one how you just met with this new guy randomly one day and now you start finding them attractive. No other words will be required. They'll burn by themselves and will do something stupid and that will be your key. Now you can put the blame on them and use that as an excuse to leave and since it doesn't bother you if they stay or leave since you already know they will because of their big self-respect. Now you can start sleeping with your new guy! And this will make them kiss bottles / die in the anger of meeting the worst person.

HAHA! writing it like if I was not the one being treated like way!

Keratin in my hair and advises for you ‘not to fall’. Got returned with light a cigarette and drink with me till you crawl. Flavor colored words were of mine but you lying was the test, even you were relying on me, It never felt like I was at my best. Should've cracked a few and left things in jest just like the first line. But I'm glad at least I followed my last three words from it.

These words don't come at an expense of nothing.
Your silence too gave me a lot of answers.

When survival was given
status became the new obsession,
like when so much time was passed
even I forgot it weren't poems
but just pain.

Drinking Potions:

' Healing:

Heal from Cold, Cough, Laryngitis

- *Small portion of ginger sliced into coins.*
- *1 tablespoon honey.*
- *1 tablespoon lemon.*
- *Teacup.*
- *Add boiling water.*
- *Mix and enjoy the soothing feeling.*

Works best when you wake up early and make it yourself. Take 3 deep breaths and exhale slowly, drink the healing potion feel it slowly sliding down your throat clearing all the negative energy.

2. Tea Sage Potion:

- *10 medium fresh sage leaves*
- *1 cup boiling water*
- *1 teaspoon lemon juice*
- *1 teaspoon honey*

G&T Potions: For the Nights

1. Pink Rose G&T Potion:

Add subtle floral taste and a smooth taste to your Gin & Tonic

- *Add 30 ml of rosewater-infused cool syrup to your drink shaker*
- *Add large ice cubes*
- *40 ml gin and 100 ml tonic water.*
- *Shake gently and pour it in a chilled glass and stir, again gently.*

Garnish with fresh rose petals and a slice of lemon.

2. Stardust Cocaine:

- *I part Bulleit bourbon.*
- *I part Amaretto.*
- *I part sparkling water*
- *Coca-cola*

Garnish with a blackberry, Stab blackberry with garnish sword. Sprinkle confection sugar on the top.

Serve over ice in rocks glass.

Bad Habits

As long as I didn't know what you really
were, it was all beautiful. Maybe that's why
*"Somethings are better not known and
somethings are better left alone."*
I wish I had gone away when I had the time.
So, today I didn't have to keep this
bad taste of you in my mouth.
Also, on rainy nights these feelings grow bigger;
I lit a cigarette from feeling being in hell, I inhale
and tried smoking you out of my lungs all the
pressure, tension started dispensing like from
smokestack on a train, It touches my lips and flees,
telling me these are the aftermath
of one not listening to their inner-self.

"Flaming sword in my right hand
tip of it depicts your dead end."

Time or people?

She makes me ride cursive
just like her body lines
hold it baby like the dam in this bridge
you gotta step away from my heart I'm
slipping down your waist line from
running nines, riding highs &
taking flights out of people's sight.
Man! Is this how we learn
- Time flies

'Jack it's not about you, I love Daniel.'

No wonder why you love kissing more bottles
than heartbreaks just cause you can't decide
whom to love and sweep &
Stop quoting Sylvia Plath, "I just want to know
everyone deeply." after you get with everyone
in those sheets like them implants ain't a scream
for 'I need more attention dweeb!'
Just be optimistic and quote, "I have an ass that
won't quit."

'Daniel it's not about you, I love...' Haha
NASTY!

Sometimes I think it was better
when I din't have you now that I do,
It doesn't make any sense now.

I keep my distance involved either rad up or let up the throttle ‘cuz for you to fuck with these vibes is to get higher than Cheech & Chong.

Getting high on Ivy,
No time on my timepiece,
Pushing drinks thru IV.
Pulling so many emotions out like
I'm swimming in it like Rikako Ikee

Switching gears, final drive, full speed
even if I'm bound to crash I finna make it a
sight-seeing.

"It's never 'leaving' when you got each other in your thoughts."

Wrote this quote on May 26, 2019. 3:44 AM

Never knew this day will come when we will not have each other in our thoughts. All the memories coming back of a person who was there helping you pack your bags last year and how tonight these hands feel weak gathering all the stuff knowing you can't put memories back. I don't know how to say goodbye to a person I never want to leave. I don't know why we got caught up in this because it's something I'm tired of experiencing again & again and tonight I don't want to see the good that comes with your 'leaving'. Tonight is just when it feels heavy on the heart. On days when it's hard to walk alone only if I could tell. The same places don't seem to be the same anymore. 'I wish you were here.' But then this statement is something I can't hold on to longer knowing...

June 22,2020

Cont.

Bratz

Caused so much turbulence
they called me a nuisance,
A new sense ever since.

And accuse me,
for abusing
when you only capable of causing a lewd scene.
So, excuse me
As I put you aside like 'few things'.

Reorganized my restrains
So, wait as I introduce me.
A thunder is yet to be stricken
& it’s my reign (rain) so you’ll hardly be missed,
even though you disgust me
when it'll hit you
you won't be even able to fart about it.

'Cuz 'light' still travels faster than sound.
And they call me 'Yagami' no wonder why
you get killed every time I write about it.

HYPNO

Marshall Bruce Mathers III

“They want me to give a ‘fuck-less’ for
doing too much if that’s so, for anyone
telling me I just gave alot too many
‘I haven’t thrown my knife anywhere
infact I sleep with ‘em every night.”

Dear Readers :

Where you going? Leaving without reading my content
not enough to make you stay? Oh! there's a picture of your
bae that's the way you wanna run,
that's the type you wanna slay?

I think I had enough of my fun, it's my time to play (shit)
Lets trade my ink with your life there's still more sense in my
game. Maybe if I revealed more skin you were more likely to
stay but nah You just gonna come (cum?) to it and go away.

It's not a one night stand !
Like my best friend getting fucked by someone else because
that's all she can. Best friend? Best fuckin end! (yeah)

That's probably why I'm here to stay as long as I've
something to say. I'm not putting my pen down
So don't ask me to put my pant down. (bitch),

fuck it !

-Regards

PratZ

-Cont.

***" While I'm writing this
You'd be sleeping with someone else."***

Things that I kept till myself.
No wonder I slept on it but couldn't sleep on my own because of it (7 months!)
Now guess who's back with it, with the same diabolical mind that ignored the vinous signs (black dahlia!). "In meantime this verse will cut you worse than you did to 7-9 others and still be stuck with the best rhyme and this bitch can suck anyone's anytime (dick?) nah peace of mind, here's a piece of mine (where?) right where I want you to be in; intertwined between these lines. guess 'it's always going to be a meantime'." (Get it?)

What a great view having you by my side to watching you walkby to someone else's view but what a bitch you'd be if you just stayed right there. So you moved from there too, to always 'being someone else's someone else boo'.

"Hey! hypno she's the one you wrote a prose for that she deleted for a new guy? haha!"

-PratZ

HYPNOTIC SPELLS

Where's your boyfriend now huh bitch? fuckin 4 lettered fuck. Oh! my bad, you'll find someone new to fuck him up and screw all you gotta do is walk outta room with your cleavage bloomed.

"Get in, get out
Fuck in, fuck out."
Reality behind your 'fuck this and fuck that'!
Done with live in? let's live out!

How's your new 'bitch made man'?
Oh! It's just a date, to the mountains just to fuck him up on the top this tongue twister faced guy of yours. Shit! That's a new score. How do I get to know, your ceilings are my floor.
But I never would've thought I'd be referring you with this shit that 'you just Bitch with the 'B' silent in it.'
And you'll be the perfect definition of
"We just met and I just fucked you."

Like that's the kind of access you have to give,
'Live the fucked up life and make it shine on social platforms.'
Hats off but
you'll never be at the same pedestal as I'm on
so F - off &
Thanks for your support Asshole !

Regards - Prat Z

As long as I'm alive and you're breathing
I'll diss you that means one of us needs
to die like 2020 but then again 'it's just a
number' like in your list of lovers.

Doing a little more for I know nothing is gonna hit back taking a stake to my heart and getting comfortable as it fits there! But till when?
What you gonna do when the heart isn't going to be there? Are you gonna stab back at the ones you loved the most?
She was already dating your friends when she was with you, nothing is going to happen just to scream, "Fuck You!". I can still stand toe to toe asking, "Wasn't I enough?" and you still can't say, 'No'.
All the hard-ships I sailed; your bullshit is the thanks I get!

And it's a quite come back with this name 'Hypno', ain't no? But what the fuck you know. Nothing has changed!
What you gonna do, When your friends tell, "You have a bad attitude, you just walk out of the room like you haven't got a clue.
You're mass confused,
inevitably screwed."

Yea, maybe I am! 'Cuz It's the same I've been.
It's just hard to tell that it's a different case I'm in.
Playing a clown since '04 hoping they are gonna do something for me though
But they just screamed 'Encore'.

"Your fans aren't always gonna be your
fans" that's what the line says.
They are there till they're benefitted from the shit
they can't grab.
The moment you're out of your context, they find
someone next,
someone new to follow up and grew.
Yea, you better stay with that one, 'Cuz you too
dumb you can't even do that to no one.
And look you got yourself into this again,
What the Fuck Mr Kain!

Freaky Tale

It's funny what I act and what I am
hate just made me a psychopath.
But I use this bullshit to my advantage,
So, I just need a knife, then I'm gonna
murder some females,
drawing on her body leaving some decals.
Your body parts look good when derailed.
No, I didn't fail to make you embarrass in my
freaky tales. This mind is asinine, so please beware.

And if you love mystery, so let this creep in your
head till you can't sleep.
Let's make you high without the Mary Jane like me,
repeating these lines to repeat black dahlia's case
for the second time in my mind, I've to ignore these
vinous signs or maybe I should spread that smile a
lil' bit in a Glasgow style.

PS: Read 'Bout 'Black Dahlia' for a crazy night.

Relief

Your judgment is something I don't need
when you know nothing about
easy to sound cocky & point out that
I act dumb, in dool
but I just act this way only in front of you
just to confuse you hoe,
I play my ace when you don't have the slightest clue.
So, Boo who?
Yea, Fuck You!
You do me no good so get out my view
that's all I wanted to
but sometimes I just can't so I have to live with you.
But I want my past crew; one more day spent with my
'Bru' can help things go to snooze.
'Cuz the place I'm in is where my ex should be and it's an
ecstasy

Cont.

that I've to keep ‘cuz saying ‘No’ doesn't help fix
weep. I don't wanna go down the same memory
lane just to remind me again the fact that you
were flat so you flip flapped on my shit just to
succeed.
Like a rolling top to reach the notch
else I'm here writing this in front of you
& BITCH! This is not for you,
this is for me.
Even if you don't like this,
I've to say
these 'Cuz
MOTHERFUCKERS
THIS IS MY
RELIEF !

Let's pick from where Hypno left off
Hypno might not have the guts to say things
But I do!
And what you thought my mother is suffering
from cancer so I won't say shit!
Since when you started to give a fuck about that?
When you left me for the dead
and I'll show you what it feels like.
As I put my dick in your mouth and break your jaw
just to make you visualize how it hard it feels like.
So, this is no story book ending,
this is only the beginning.
& what you thought I ran out of words? (Huh!)
Got more than your CV ever will.
Laughing behind my back like I can't see that?
Got myself blacking out. Now see me reflecting in the knife.
I will cut the utmost with it
I mean you & I'm here to take my respect back.
Making them clean on all the mess under your pressure
they used the same broom to fly off.
I aspired from it no wonder why it hurts yours eyes now
from all the knives you put in my hind end are now the
reason why I will write till your dying end.
Bitch! I'm not gonna make you look good on this side
(You not a cuisine!) My will I'm imposing &
this is only for those who I'm inspiring.

Intro

I aint coming yet.
I'll come in a minute (Okay)
It's not easy to make me cum (Wtf P.?)
It's a formal book you can't just put whatever you want in it!
Uh huh? Tell me about it.
"The weight of your rear end might be too much for you to carry around want me to hold it for you?" Is that how you formally ask when you wanna grab some ass?
Inappropiate?
So be it! The best part about me is I'm not you I'm me.
Lemme grab my phone.

Dials
Yo, Bru!
Waddup champ?

Just a funny thought came to my mind to appreciate you when I still can. You my best hype man thanks for climbing my gate that day man definitely opened a lot more door than just that one & I got your back dawg.
Now let's get this one (You got this bruv.)

What I feel now is I should strike first and ask 'em to reverse 'TIKCUS' afterwards to see what this unsigned hype does. I got a halo too on top of my head until I took my last fall and bent the damn the thing. So, I broke the damn ring in two, upswinged it from both ends (wink). Now I got two horns that don't honk (Beep-Beep). That's why I can't stay censored (Get it?) Beep-Beep
Fuck it!

CLAIRE

Hey! Claire, How have you been doing?
You've not been texting me lately are you not feeling
me on the inside (oh!) I mean on the out. Shit! I'm in the
mood again. So mighty and nuisance;
I'm the same on the inside and out: Hard.
Oops! I mean call me translucent.
Brain's nuts like I've been ruthlessly bent somewhere
between my hippocampus & cerebellum.
What a perfect example of having 3 personalities bursting
out from one! Fighting to see who you gave head to first
Tryna get me off?
Get me off this cunt!
I only get off when my lines hit harder than guillotine style.
Sophomore, when we were together, fast forward to the last
year, now I say, hand me the saw amore just like my last
whore, I gotta keep coming back for more like the blades on
this chainsaw. I said,
I keep coming back like the blades on this chainsaw.
So, that's where I attack from.
How can I quit when my haters haven't? (yeah)
I speak the truth, always giving complex to these
Bitches (oops), hoes, I mean whores.
Excuse my language I'm 'Munchausen by proxy'
making you sick to your head, but I was just giving you back
what you were giving back to everyone (giving head!)
But like you,
I'm also here to entertain!

Innocent Bystanders

No one appreciates a person whose self-esteem
is shot the hell up and they are falling helplessly.
So, I can't even say that what kind of a man I'd be
If I can't even stand on my own, let alone standing
on my own & looking for myself but
that's just not enough to make 'em proud of that!
Saying, "What's our fault if he is an introvert so he
doesn't have any friends, he's a loner so he can't stay
here for much longer, he's a goner." (True!)
But for you to strip me of my confidence:
Mission unaccomplished!
So, even If you compare me to a mutt (bitch!)
You don't want my claws to come out &
I'mma make sure, It's gonna hurt like you
got bit by a K9 (canine). Because,
"Forgive and forget is the only thing I'd ever live to regret!"

Curtain Call

Give me accelerants, cocaine, explosive agents &
propane. Bring it all in, for some of y'all are gonna
like me & some ain't and that's okay!
I'm not here even dizzy bizzy, teeny weeny, miny
moe to make y'all like me, I'm done with that shit.
So, bite me!
But, I'm so cute for y'all to dislike me (Haha!)
So, let's come back, dive in to the start and just like me!
Surprising?
I'm still enticing!

(Hypno: Leave the world alone this ain't their fault you
don't have to be rude about that.
PratZ: Fuck that! Call 911! This is the terror attack, call it
9/11 isn't that the same day when I was born, 9th Nov.)

I remember when I was smol my teacher used to
compare me with a crow or a rat till that bitch had a son
that looked like an asshole! After 8th it got worse before
it was more but I did not have the voice to say it in front
of y'all. To this day,
I keep ramming in absurd people like my legs are drunk
and brain is blindfolded nowhere to go from here to
dump this baggage till I learned to take it all in, mixed it
bad in duffle bags and took out a baseball bat and swung it
as hard as I can that it made all your senses flat and said,
"Guess who's back?"

Gasket

As the sun sets, Smirnoff is out and on.
In my Monte Carlo approaching rendezvous,
too many exit points to begin with too many
rhinestones to strike with and I'mma wear all of 'em (Why?)
cause why not? (self-made haha!).
Look at me, the definition of what it feels to sip wine on
Saturday night (Ah, shit!) that's Hypno. I'm what a knife
feels like in your guts & at the same time what's it like
when your mind is deep throated and stapled to your
nuts. In other words, "I give no fucks!"
& look at you, a fan of that.
I was prepared for this so, props to me for being a gasket &
holding too much at once so,
even in the dark, I hit like if I'm the night (knight)
& don't worry I'm moving on to bigger and better than
things and I don't mean no dicks, I'm not that bitch!
On my way to success like these words on this paper,
'I'm looking up'. Stop me if you think it takes a whole
squad of swat to get me off and I'd still be coming back
swinging like a pendulum in this game & even if you
are good at killin' time, you are the only one who'll be
getting killed that's what it is like to go against me.
My lines are 3 am cravings so that's a food for thought.
Let's see how long it takes for you to digest, I mean,
catch on every phrase, before you miss out on sleep.
(Now that's a longing!)

Friends

"For a fact, I know the people with me might
not be the same behind my back, but to care for that
shit – I still hold the power."

There's nothing left in me in the name of a friend
and everything that relates on...
So, fuck off!
This is 'The Potion Store', I'm here to store y'all
and use your brains combined to write
the dopest lines – that's why you like my shit
'cuz I've already said the things that are on your minds.
Now you wanna get in my brain?
Well, I just had breakfast with Viagra.
So, I think with my dick in this game.
You gonna be realizing,
what I'm doing is re-wiring,
'even if I'm nuts, you're still below me.'
With every page, I'm upscaling,
re-styling, re-rhyming,
freestyling and think of me as Bizarre or Shady with Dre beats
blaring 'In my head' screaming 'Still Aftermath' &
'Still Shady chick!'
Props to the greatest other words, this is also a tribute as they
continue their legacy, giving freedom to so many.
If it wasn't for Shady I would've never been able to throw my
first punch and still can and this is one of 'em!
So, thank you for changing my childhood M&M's
to bigger treats, thank you Marshall for also becoming Eminem.

Fin.

Visit me on
Instagram: @hypnospells

www.ingramcontent.com/pod-product-compliance
Lightning Source LLC
LaVergne TN
LVHW070843160826
845684LV00008B/58